IN THE LILAC HOUR

and other poems

IN THE LILAC HOUR

and other poems

John Muro

Antrim House
Bloomfield, Connecticut

Library of Congress Control Number: 2020941377

ISBN: 978-1-943826-71-1

First Edition, 2020

Printed & bound by Ingram Spark

Book design by Rennie McQuilkin

Front cover artwork by Michael Muro

Antrim House
860.217.0023
AntrimHouseBooks@gmail.com
www.AntrimHouseBooks.com
400 Seabury Dr., #5196, Bloomfield, CT 06002

This book is dedicated to Debra Ann.

Acknowledgements

Grateful acknowledgement to the editors of the Guilford Poet's Guild 20th Anniversary Anthology, *Our Changing Environment, 2019*, in which "Swainson's Thrush" first appeared.

I am also grateful to Susan F. Murray and the late Hugh Ogden for their unconditional support and encouragement; to friends and family, both past and living, who have been a source of support and inspiration; and to my son, Michael, for developing the book's cover art.

Special thanks to Rennie McQuilkin: advocate, sponsor, publisher, friend.

TABLE OF CONTENTS

Fore-words

Gli Uccelli

In Memoria

I Fiori

Il Mare

After-words

Writing at random – straining at particles of light
in the midst of a great darkness.

– John Keats

IN THE LILAC HOUR

and other poems

FORE-WORDS

The Undoing

October now is four weeks in,
Scent of woodsmoke's upon the wind;
And my wooden ladder's thin
Rails are set hard against the eaves.

It takes more than faith to begin
This task, for the way of wind
On autumn days is contrarian –
Will soon replace the eight-penny leaves

I've lifted, scarlet stems pinned
Deep within the primordial resin
Where fallen worlds soften
From shingle stone. They sink by degrees.

If left to wind, none of these would ascend
From the fetid sediment, nor the fin-
Like leaves, serrated, half-settled in
The throat of downspouts. Nearby trees,

From roofline, still hold to green
And gold. The weathervane's
Copper ship banks west again,
Cutting across a lichened sea.

I too must move. Having harvested enough of sin
I balance myself and then begin
A final uprooting, toward absolution.
I descend more warily.

Searching for Blue

Sunlit fingers uninvited come
Prying open windows,
Turning out bedquilts
And rearranging the larder;
Winter-weary eyes lift from earth
And the garden's stubble.

The season we're turning from
Was long in leaving and slow
To stray. All things blue wilted,
Including the sky. All was harder
And hardened; a still-birthed
Season from which we still stumble.

Above eaves, ice-laden gutters run;
Cold is easing. A near-liquid flow
Of water and snow-matted
Stones that will fall back to yard.
Most are small in girth,
Red-brown and umber.

There's beauty in the undone
And the unkempt, though.
Consider the orphaned crow's
Dull sheen; search is harder,
Surely, but blue's uncovered
Hearing with eyes half full.

Restoration

All becomes more alien as we age;
The life we inhabited is lifted; set apart;
Something known, but strange,
Giving way to a slow,
Certain ending.

The mind is dumbstruck; and the rage
Fixed within this frail, four-chambered heart
Fades to cold; orange
Embers once glowing
Now are abiding

Ash. Wants matter so very little now;
The loam-rich earth and foam-flecked sea
Call to us,
But diminished senses still
Deny

The brute turning out of a life ill-spent; bowed
And broken; a raw, frail design too easily
Frayed brimming with decay and rust.
Fragments all too easily settling –
To field or foam.

Enter, then, with steps long and slow,
And revive this aging heart;
Let me, for once, feel as though –
However uneasily –
Life's been worth trying.

March Wants for Ornament

March wants for ornament,
Something heaven-sent:
Purpling dusk, a crescent
Moon of crushed gold; bent

Skies of indelible blue. Sprays
Of lavender. On such days,
Memory is tested and weighted
Without the means to color or phrasing.

Beyond the crow's raucous ache
Or the gathering gray and breaks
Of earth in black-brown spackle,
Thawings of creosote that crack

Crust and are thrown up in gruesome displays,
Like relics, of how deep an endless winter cuts.

Summer Idyll

A long weekend worth savoring, she said,
A truce was struck, we buried our dead.
Overhead, beneath the eave, a spiderweb,
An abscess of pearl, a hard husk, bled
Of life; a fleck of leg or wing, chaff spread
To edge, a billowing tomb of red
I could not keep my eyes from. I read
That the long departed and newly dead
Provide for us; no longer weighed by fear,
The shriveled corpse, thru nickel-clear
Silk, takes up its Elysian lyre,
And with wind whispers eerily to ear
Of corruptible flesh and such unbearable
Tragedies yet to come in later years.

In This Hour of Respite

In this hour of respite
Tangled in drooping dark,
Porch lights turning out,
Stars brittle-bright glint.

Frail senses wander,
Spy the flitting black
Smudge of bats; crack
Of doors that linger

Long on pneumatic air;
Pondside, the muffled plop
Of a kingfisher, perhaps,
Pitched clear

Of willow. Lavender
Scents from the gardens
Drift past; a distracted wren
Discerned in a queer

Shaft of moonlight.
Relief meant to mean
Something between
The darkness and light.

I Do

A quiet,
Near-holy light;
Sky,
An undefiled blue.
Bouquets
Of pink and purple
Roses,
Some askew,
Adorn each row;
A soft dusk
Of globed grapes
And berries blush
Linen tables.
It's Saturday.
Soft shouldered
Waves – shades
Of oyster gray
And cobalt blue.
Sea spray plumes
Leap then falter;
Wind
Waits,
Finds its way
To gossamer skirts
And altar.
The bride's
A friend's daughter.
Procession hesitates.
A harp glissando,
Like trickling water,

Shudder of violins.
Near the driveway
(Not out of view)
A quartet of crows,
Unwilling to wait,
Make feast
Of a dying stray,
An ill-timed repast.

Among These Acres Now Gone Green

for my brother, Joseph

Among these acres now gone green
Summers lingered long with leaf
And honeysuckle days were spent
Among teeming boughs bent
By wind, sweetly scented, drifting
About the lilacs and in between
Forts and fields and a slow
Stream purling like inklings to ear;
Sun like tinsel caught in the wings
Of dragon flies and glistening
From the slap of trout clearing
The stream's tea-colored narrows.

Summer eyes feigned sleep and ached
For light and day's long, languid arc
Across a sky of baptismal blue.
Setting out, spears and arrows were hewn
From branches of maple and ash
Even as dew's pebbled glaze lingered;
And on days of rain we rushed
To brooding barn and scents of leather,
Dry hay and coal; honey brown bales
Were barriers of stubble to breach
And push past. In warmer weather,
We'd return to pause of pasture

And the pond with bottomless bays
Where a wooden skiff was moored; lines
Lifted and we were in pursuit of the kraken;
Submerged limbs were tentacles hidden

In its wet labyrinth of leaves and vines
Before a slow retreat into hydrangea shade.
At night, fireflies, winking like stars,
Were pursued, too, as gilded treasure
Before the loud, persistent calls
From screen doors and the weighted lull
As cunning minds measured
The cost of prolonging nocturnal wars.

Clotheslines, susceptible to wind,
Served to divide fair from foul
Laundered walls we might fall against,
Incurring fractures from a fence
Of billowing sheets and towels,
A tangle of green and linen white.
On rarer days, we planned our ascent
Of forgotten hill and the reservoir
Beyond. Our trailhead was a cluster
Of pines, frothing pools of rusted
Needles. Prickly cones stored,
We passed deep channels of fern

And clouds of resin. Frayed ropes,
Made from vines, were set
And used for cords and harness.
All about us twilight's tarnish
And fallen limbs, like frets,
We stumbled up uneven slopes.
Upon return, bikes were cutters on seas
Lapping ballfields and cliffs of sand.
Ashore, we leapt heavenly and headlong
Into cascading waves of gritty foam.
Such sublime journeys in joy ended
With dwindling indolence and ease.

At Twelve

How is it
I still recall
The girl
Wearing
A white dress,
Gold-brown
Hair tangled
In a drizzled stem
Of purple
Lilacs as day
Was darkening?
Light was weak,
But I caught the all of her
(She was not alone;
Her younger sister
Sat on swing;)
I must confess
To a certain dawdling
Until pressed
To approach her.
A car idled,
A voice called.
Unflattering,
She released the branch
Absentmindedly
And turned
To slow shadow
As the bush drifted
And I was left,
After a few steps,

In sweet retreat,
Three friends teasing
When I pedaled home
Grateful for her leaving.
Yet, how many times
I returned to find
That lost kiss or signs
Of darkest purple blossoming.

April's Autumn

Were this day a flower surely it would be
An orchid opening in gilded leisure, petals
As opulent as an oriole in undulating flight;
The rose-orange underlip of cloud – sepals
Laden with the wet of fragrant light –
Bloom from mottled beds of sphagnum and sea.
From a later sky, a Pentecost pours,
Blue-speckled, through this push of petals
And musky warm of autumn. Plumes of green-gold
And ochre quiver in exquisite alchemy –
A fragmentary fuss of light and wind that holds
Sky to land like an epiphyte until from this blaze of shore
We've never been more certain of how delicate and cold
The distance between life and death and something more.

Good Humor Man

The only emperor is the emperor of ice-cream.
— Wallace Stevens

Sprinkling icicle clang and cymbal-clear clatter,
The logo-laden calliope conjures a sweet soup
Of voices – the tinkling chime of bicycle bells,
The screak and yelp of door-slap and hurried
Footfall in sneakered rush no sooner settling
Than the chirr of currency and change, coaxed
From fluted nooks is muffled in bundles
Of open palms and fingers. Now, all eyes heed
The broad yawp and squeal of tabernacle hinge
Flaking to butter-gold and rum; the slow curdle
Of dry-ice mists and holy plunder of eclairs and
Ices, shortcakes and cones, and one by one the
Ladled lift of cold confections taken
To air like eucharists before a harlot moon.

for dad, mom, brothers and sis

Gilead

On such a day as November might own,
A sunless sky of nickel-gray
And brooding clouds piling up like slabs
Of stone,

I set out alone
Into the outer dark where wind stabs
At easy flesh and the pathway
Towards the woods (typically overgrown
With bone-

White birch and oak) is near-leafless;
Some, with silvered undersides, appear
Like stiff fish curled and cracked
By air.

Past the hoary undergrowth, I pass
Into the higher pastures where
Shards of gold fracture
The air

And heavy crowns dip earthwards
From the weight of a sun-bright harvest;
And tongue upon orange tongue
Stir

The air with a crisp rustling that springs
Around us – and so lingers. Now, hope is tested.
A winter-long darkness and too few birds
And woods

Left to me alone. Eyes empty and overtired,
I sense the sudden onset of snow;
My steps homeware slow
Knowing more than half a life's expired.

Danaë

How might lust best create
A form ineffable, transmute
From flesh-bound cloud into
A blinding light that bathed

Her form in resplendent grace?
No arms or lips were placed
Upon her; a glittering deluge
Of straw-gold light burned through

To marrow, encircling limbs and face
In the sweet ravishing. The exquisite taste
Of flaxen light as her lips withdrew
In ecstasy. Air burned back to blue.

A strange, intoxicating alchemy
Devoid of touch, fragrance or memory.

In the Lilac Hour

In the lilac hour,
The growing green season slows;
The ache to fruit and flower
Recedes. The want to grow,

For a time,
Gives way to a soft easing
And a divine
Purpling of grass and trees.

Wind is quelled,
The mellifluous sparrow,
The tumbled crunch of gravel
Underfoot, hushed; the glow

Of oriole-bright lanterns,
Displaces a moon of shook foil,
Stars in leaf-bowed branches burn
And burn; ash drifts to soil.

A damp fragrance lingers,
Grafts to tongue
And so, to ear, creak of hinge
From the garden gate.

Remembering
Now, the brighter blur,
The quickening of things,
Before the ever after.

Portent

Decades apart, the mother stands,
Dutifully places the plastic instruments
Upon the tray filled with bottled lotions
And oils; drapes the time-worn blanket
From shoulder to knees and gathering strands
Of her daughter's hair, sets in motion

The near-sensual sweep of brush and comb;
Applies the spray of topaz wash while
Avoiding the mid-day light and faces
Captured in stark, yet wistful, profile
And perhaps wonders how, years from now,
Chair-bound, she might yet recall traces

Of such kind labors, the small blue tangle
Of forget-me-nots, her daughter's name
Or the purpose of the linen blanket
Enveloping her shrunken frame
And the distant sounds of angels
Amid those brute yet simple instruments.

Confession

Pre-dawn, a holy stillness
Falls. The forest hoards
And harbors silence
Beneath boughs
Bent in genuflection,
Their girth grafted
From the strata of early snow.

Darkness is tethered,
Awaits the inexorable tumble
That follows the soft jostle by wind;
That could be hours,
Or days, from now
And I court the emptiness;
A bird's call, dying on the wing.

Little else I bring
Beyond a winter weariness;
A solitary crow,
Serif set upon a branch, flowers
Into flight: a half-thought, a sin
Denied, even as I stumble
Into this darkest of weathers.

Clouds closing, row upon row,
Thick pleats of cloth, ill-crafted,
Muffle the contrition
That comes from below
These ministrations: recompense
For the divide between what's been done
And what was intended. Surely less.

Homecoming

for my sons and daughter

Miles from the interstate
Tucked within a tiny hollow
Of bittersweet and stunted pine
The country store
Beckoned with a pool
Of mid-day light
Passing thru the
Leaded glass
Of weathered windows;
A warped, wafer-thin door,
Listing and dreaming plumb.
A brief pause for
Balance before
The imperceptible sinking
Into floorboards sole-worn
And strangely bowed,
And ancient shelves
Brimming with penny
Purchases of confections
And dusty cases
Of colored bottles –
Pungent candles of
Paraffin: cardinal
Red, daylily orange and
A stable-straw yellow –
And beyond the narrow
Aisles the recesses
Of dank solitude
And eerie silhouettes

Where a young boy,
Freckled from summer
Sun and subject to
Strange imaginings,
Lingered for a time
And took in these
Random scents
Of wet wood, resin,
Plaster and hay,
Stabbing at memory
Moments before
The eager footfall,
A bat and glove
Balanced
On handlebars –
Shock of silver
As bright as lightning –
Then the soft spank
Of the thin door
Closing upon
A childhood swaddled
And carried into
Further worlds
Both familiar
And foreboding.

Wormsloe

for Carmine

We half expect to see the mournful ferry,
Docked in daylong dryness at the channel's end,
Where the water is bone dust lapping and Charon
Eases an empty skiff to motion with his pole.
Beneath the canopy, one sees less clearly
Where branches open; an ashen-blue blends
With a fluid, playful light that turns upon
The air. Apparitions, perhaps, of displaced souls
With gilded coins where veils of dust appear;
And, there, pensive Persephone's descending
A sloping path of whorled shells and sand
Towards Acheron and the unlit intervals
Of lamentation beneath these wounded boughs where
Light dissolves in passage and Furies take to air.

My Athena

for Susan Fenton Murray

For it was she who cleared
The dark debris in
That garden, weed-filled,
Nurturing the few flowers
Worth tending and
Coaxing to sun:
A kind of blossoming.

Tempered and channeled fear
Long-nurtured, its origin
Buried deep, well-tilled,
Taste the tenor and allure
Of iridescent strands
And light: vistas un-
Fathomed yet beckoning.

Taught how best to hear
And take in
Meaning – the quiet thrill
In later hours –
Of euphony and certain
Phrases turning
And a want to sing.

A Day in April

Spring sky so clear one might see
The calm nestled deep inside the blue;
Light-footed birds drifting across
Hushed air and a pathless sea
Slowly ebbing, birthing fewer
Waves. The shoreline's pressed

To glimmering silt. Salt-thick smell
Mingles with the drunken light
Stumbling from wave to wave;
The drop of moon, a bleached shell,
Still hews to the bluer edge of night
As it withers to windward dawdle:
Marvels at the wonder of this day
And grace unfathomable.

Montagne Sainte-Victoire

(Paul Cezanne, 1905-1906)

It was opulently set,
His Parnassus,
With luminous palette
Vast, yet intimate,
A heaven woven
And shaped by light;
Blue bleeding white
Diaphanous
As if it were of the air
Distance draws near,
Revealing
Shimmering truths:
A landscape
Linen,
Porcelain,
Clear.

Still Life with Fruit

i

A bouquet of fruit perched
Upon a beveled platter of glass;
A table laden and gold light's grazing
The studied jumble of mingled mass.

ii

Pomegranates, placed towards the ends
Are berms of mottled burgundy and heather;
Their small chimney stems appear black
With soot; their flesh the texture of coarse leather.

iii

Brood of green-gold grapes, dew-
Glistening, as if with specks of mica, over-
Lay broad boulders of apple, freckled skin
Kindled by the deflected light of trickling water.

iv

Orphan peach, brushed with rouge, hint of coral
Blossoming, and likely the first to blister
And shed its skin; bruise of plural plums, violet-yellow,
Abandoned lanterns that flicker and dissolve to mist.

V

Gold-green intrusion of oblong pear, a tilted
Buddha, bulging bauble given to girth, would be first
To plummet into the pool of fabric below:
A sleeping serpent coiled in blue burnish.

Midday Moon

A midday moon
I mistook
For a cyst of cloud,
A heron's loud-
White wing,
Clipping wind;
A peony blossom
Wind forgot
To bring
Back to earth.
Blue-birthed
And over-worn,
A dreamless
Face, mid-yawn,
With rolled back eye,
A pallid display
In mid-day sky
That I'd try
To make whole again,
But then,
Even worldly
Pilgrims lose
Their way
Late and early.

Rainbow Trout

The wonder is so small a stream could sustain
The thing: a stone submerged or limb fixed in
Undertow, until the slow, effortless sweep of tail
Pushed it deftly past shadow and it flared out
Towards a pool of light, the slosh and prattle
Of braided water refracting its mottled flesh –
Brittle-gold phosphorous and a bloom of pink –
Before it drifted sideways beneath foam and a tangle
Of roots as if it were prepared to wait out
The season in stellar calm; and then once
Again in liquid torpor it transformed itself –
A late leaf fallen or tinseled flutter of writhing
Weed engulfed in a blush of melt waters
As dark and dense as any dusk or drowning.

Rose's Farm

Bolton, CT

We could not have imagined the heartache
Of this place, the farmhouse rising from
Or tumbling towards that lap of porch
Bearing the weight of weather and haunted
Footfall of generations spent tending
Hillside pasture. Lifetimes ago, they
Must have watched the seasons wash
Across this land in need of perpetual
Healing, and perhaps with prodding,
Mended the sprawl of oval stone
And the wooden throat of silo.
Farther out, where light leaks
Through cloud, the frothy bloom
Of orchards in opal air; the brooding
Beech abiding, with its trembling tapestry
Of sun and leaf and air, the punctuated
Spirals of swallows taking to a sky
Thickening with the damp of hay
And grape and the drowsiness that
Comes from a long-labored settling.

*Rose's Farm consists of over 100 acres
of land. It was purchased by the
Town of Bolton in 2000, and is now
preserved as part of Bolton Heritage
Farm.*

GLI UCCELLI

Crow

More astonished than perturbed
By the sudden jolt of black,
The bold abundance of wings
Melting from the lower eaves,
I am struck by the unadorned moxie
Of flagrant theft, the deftness
Of his pick-pocket pilfering
Of straw from the flower box: bird
Eerily contorted and capsized
With tail feathers raised, his back
Turned from his base enterprise
And expert eye transfixed on us.
Readily acknowledging his audacity,
With beak brimming full, he returns to nest.

Swans of Leete's Island

As if fallen from high, heavy clouds
And idly set upon the water
They're spectacles of feathered opulence

In an inlet of pewter-blue. Too loud
White, they appear as porcelain
Bowls of delicate design. Their curved

Napes decline and elegantly ladle
Dollops of cream into water.
Devoutly following

In impossible buoyancy, a cumulus
Rush blown to shore, blowsy
Blossoms

Untethered by wind. Bills are bright coals
Burning as if they'd somehow alter
Their conspicuous splendor.

Egrets are flushed from shoals
Littering trees as the exotic squatters
Drift past in languid amble.

As furtive as purple loosestrife, flowering rush
Or dense milfoil, they dissemble
In dormant drift, clamorous

Wings idled in dense, feathered folds
Of plumage, foregoing clearer waters

To claim this sanctuary of crusted

Ice. Cloud or blossom or snow,
Canopies by season alter.
Delighted eyes are easily bewitched.

Among Monarchs

A thing incorporeal
Epaulet of oriole
And element of ether;

Rubbled chrysalis
In translucent flourish
Is either

Bittersweet burst
Or ghostly citrus
Borne to air.

Wafted brooch adorns
Whorls of lavender
Starry plumes of aster

Wings recast as petals,
Or diaphanous shells
Fox-orange flare;

Amalgam of wing and tongue
Folded hinge hung
In a queer

Fancy. Lifters of grief,
A straw-spun gold leaf
Or flickering ember.

Effortless ascension,

A sylph's spirit spun
From terrestrial life

To one that's wind-borne
Soft-leaved hushed,
Orange-gold-amber crushed;

Underwings lift and repulse
Gravity and ineloquence
In froth of air.

Wood Thrush

September 11, 2001

In thinning light, the loose assembly
Of leaves and shadow closes in,
The catbird's shrill prattle
From the under story has ceased.

Above us, where air is creased,
Tucked and folded by wind,
All sound and motion settle;
From the far side of the canopy,

A song, flute-like, effortlessly eased
To ear, oblate in texture, begins
Low, rises and too quickly tumbles
To deeper silence and memory.

Near-light is extinguished. Then
The slow, deliberate assembly
Of stars set between the cruel,
Late gathering of leaves

And we are left with only
The sweet call-note as daylight ends
And a heaven mourns. Our hearts,
Having savored joy, now run full with grieving.

Hermit Thrush

Careworn from days convulsed by sun
And the stale heft of midsummer air,
We hear a healing pour from where
Rows of sweet birch run
To darkness but still ladle light.

Dry waves of wind pick up, reveal
An intermittent flash of plumage;
Gigue-quick fluster amid foliage
Or feather flared to sorrel,
Green to brown and white.

Hours tossed in tumult seem to settle
And hold apace; we are content
To remain here for a moment,
Perhaps an hour until
The soft withdrawal of light.

Sensing this, an easeful cadence
Tumbles to earthbound ear;
Woodlands, in turn, appear
To ache in silence –
Sound displaces sight.

The permeable down of song
Comes to nest in us,
Melts shade to solace –
The timbre of other tongues
In dappled light.

A sudden slap and flurry of wings,
Branches blur in fitful bustle;
Bird now indistinguishable
From leaves; something
Of or from the night.

Swainson's Thrush

The long, slow glide
That took them through
The narrow channel of light,
Wedged between the weeping
Beech and tides of astilbe
Foam, ended here with
The full brunt of glass
That they could not push past.
Out of earshot, I did not
Hear the hollow boom
And dull thud that followed;
Or the pillows of autumn air part
And the headlong fall
Into the drab olive wash
I mistook for moss
And found not one,
But two, mere weeks apart:
One by the garden's edge,
The other, perhaps with
Pain unpartnered, a few
Feet distant, and there
I clasped this second, slender
Self and marveled at
The lack of heft, the
Very ease with which
The feathers and speckled
Body folded into my hands,
The tiny head toggling
Loosely back and forth
Like a browning fruit.

I was unable to heal the rupture
Of body from bone,
Cruelly uncentered,
That once launched, from woodland shadows,
A spiraling, flute-like song
Before the dark grace
That fell into a sudden shock
Of silence and brief transcendence.

Birds of Youth

A sky so deep,
So suddenly blue
A portal I fell through
And nimbly tumbled
Til greeting ground –
A bed of slate –
I stumbled
Back into
A world without sound –
Sterile, chaste,
Silence grated.
About me, incurious class-
Mates
Removed from pews
And clouds of incense,
Behind confessionals of glass –
Birds brightly hued,
A precise blue,
Lapis,
Wings motionless,
Undersides bleached
With fibers of dust.
Frescoed nests, too,
And paper branches crusted
With blossoms shoddily glued
And for just
A moment, a cruel
Indulgence –
Air jeweled,
Bright and merciless.

Fool's Gold

A May afternoon in want of light,
And you wondered how so many
Blossoms could possibly fall and
Flood the air; but it was a sudden
Squall of snow, a season fraying
As if winter wished to remain
Something more than memory.
And later that day, with borrowed
Skies returned to sun, a more
Gruesome visitation – a mutant
Gull spilled like flotsam
Into our yard, its wing dragging
Behind its broken body
Like a tangled kite,
Then the sudden, choreographed
Descent of coal-black snow –
Three crows clothed in hunger
And a shared understanding
Of what truly binds them –
Found their way to grass,
Their lightless, prospector
Eyes, tiny pellets of onyx,
Coldly weighing if this
Disheveled specimen –
A mute howl of spindrift –
Was fool's gold or, in fact,
Their next eureka moment.

Song Sparrow

An April morning is mere moments from blue's
First blush. Beyond the beveled glass, all's at rest
And shadows frame the first pale light. Arbors
Of blossoms could be epaulets fixed upon a sudden
Flash and flurry of wing.

This frail nub is far less accomplished and true
Than its speckled throat at song; its timbre arrests
And delights the ear, even as it calls for
A more absolute accounting of things forgotten –
Such disquiet this wild migrant brings.

Daybreak now dissolves and a watery blue
Builds beyond the horizon. A sad solace:
The limp drift of songs with fewer chords,
And a life slowed by the leaden
Weight of things.

Years are mute and will not answer, though truth
In melody comes from a higher perch, sets
And makes a life without the gift of words:
That jubilant aubade where memory, at last, opens
And the dry heart sings.

Mallards

Tucked among the rushes,
A speckled loaf of bird:
Golden-brown hen, color
Of dried tobacco leaf.
Dabbling, with flare of tail
Clearing water, the drake
Bears a sorcerer's visage
With a fluorescent head
Of ghoulish green
And a deep blue
Patch blurred to wing
As if a slice of sky
Was woven to feather.
Rowdy, gourd-orange
Legs prop up his plump
Body. He dotes for now,
Follows her step for step,
From inlet water to nest,
Knowing with brash color
Comes a sweeter song
And another mate.

Osprey

Might this be the fabled raptor
The gods chose as tormentor
Of Prometheus?

Its massive wings the size
Of a boy's body, lurid eyes
Of yellow rust

Portend the sharp talon,
The terrible tongue
And beak thrust

Into flesh, the grim price
For fire's gruesome sacrifice
That's best

Left to myth. Now, angler of air,
Wings hover and drift clear
Of marsh,

Pause, then plummet to prey,
The bird's body a fanned display
Of feathers crushed.

It returns to air with writhing fish
Held head-long thru gusts
Of wind – and us.

IN MEMORIA

For Father

And with ghastly whispers tell, that
joy, once lost, is pain. – Percy Bysshe Shelley

This morning, in need of healing,
I took the more
Desolate road to you
Along the high ridge of lake
Where pines are tall enough
To knead the fog that's as thick
As the clouds uncoupling
In this bowl. For a sudden
Moment, the surface cleared
Like a mind emptying.

As is our custom,
I dip the razor's neck, slap
The pool of porcelain in such
A way your hands instinctively
Open to catch the muffled drum
Of air. With each slow stroke
Swallowed by your cheeks
I see how your mouth has settled
Like an open wound and how the
Glad green has gone from your eyes,
Hazel leaking away, and
How it seems every part of your
Body is flaking flesh.

Remembering
A time before you came to be

In their keeping and housed
Among fresh-laundered scents –
Anticipating the arrival of a
Stillness so much different than
The life you'd led – the utter shame
Of idleness and the taking of
Something too readily offered;
A keen distrust of strangers
And too-soon smiles; an uneasy
Comfort taken only by constantly
Pushing yourself years beyond reason;
Holding to a deep-down knowing that
It is always possible to persist
Despite the blur and blending of
Seasons or young and vulnerable sorrows
Breaking in early morning when time
Holds like a breath drawn.

For Joseph Paul

Praising what is lost makes the remembrance dear
　　　　　　　　– William Shakespeare

The weight of waiting now lifted,
The sting of silence displaces
Your prolonged gaspings for air.
Alien arms and sallow cheeks
Are puddled with gray, and a body
Once long for laughing is now
Slowly spent by a grief that gives
No quarter. Curtains are sadly shut
And the scent of camphor collects
In corners, congeals and seems
To clot the air while a new anguish
Wakens and my thoughts turn to how
Best, at this hour, with all light quenched,
To nurse our grieving and somehow
Keep you even as I remember
A younger self and your way of looking
At the world as if all was bountiful
And each day a new setting out
And each hour a new occasion.
Now day fades; behind you, faint diodes
Fall like notes on a scale from green
To black to interminable black.
A prolonged cold presses in, and
I think of that other you knowing
What lies beyond is but more darkness
And unhurried days convulsed
By regrets and ill-timed mercies.

A Time of Leaving

for Linda

For a month or more it had sustained us;
That plumage of leaf, full-figured, lemon-
Gold gone brighter by the hour. We could
Only guess at when the wind would settle
And pick clean that unspent hope, leaving little
More than a gaunt carcass and a perch from
Where we might survey how it was we came here;
How at this time of leaving, you could be no
Less radiant than those epaulets of leaf that
Somehow burned on, and in, to seasons once
Prescribed to passing and befuddled the elements
As November rains fell and the air bled in
Colors that did not emerge as much as the thin
Veneer of summer imperceptibly burned away.

Elegy for Josephine

Grateful for those few hours
Spent in late November when
I came unattended to your room,
Readjusted the ill-framed picture
Of a woman in middle age
Given to grieving
With stoic spouse and a darker
Afternoon of trees large enough
To swallow all sun that was just then
Settling outside your window.
How quickly your
Small frame collapsed into itself
And how your lightless eyes
Forewarned me that a mere day
Would pass before you took to light
And I returned to gather your
Too-few belongings and stare
More intently across the years
At that brooding photograph
Where smiles and softer stares
Could just as well have been
Misgivings, and greet you with
Eyes closed and the whole hollow
Of your mouth open, ushering all
Towards some unfathomable deep
I thought stirred just above you.

I FIORI

Parrot Tulips

Each petal's a fevered stroke
In the manner of Goya or Van Gogh,
Contorted icons of the Baroque –
Perverse purple; glut of green-yellow.

Moon-sewn lips of exotic excess,
Shells of gruesome splendor,
Writhing flames of wrinkled flesh
In cruel, curvaceous flower.

A florid fusion of lust and angst,
Wilted feathers of evil delight,
A Harpy's wing detached
Hung in lurid light.

Voluptuous flutings of plumaged conch,
Gorged cusps in billowing blush.

Lobelia

Cardinal Flower

i

In the language of the garden,
They are the hyphens,
The grave accent,
Ushering sonorous
Inflections of bee hum
In pungent air.

ii

Incendiary petal flare,
The color that comes
From the arching thrust
Of fireworks in descent,
The freckled fade at ending,
Tiny sparks on time-delay.

iii

Fire walls of vibrant red
Oozing alarm,
Brightness that blinds
And ignites the breeze,
A scent of acrid smoke
Like smoldering cedar.

iv

Medicinal ember,
Who could know
These bright apostrophes
Are sedatives designed
To foster calm
And soothe the blood?

Yard Work

That mound of cedar mulch
Bleeds steam and water and
Will not have me idle.
Twelve yards worth holds
Like a hill, and on a certain
Sunday it is an oriole's perch
That impales me to loam
Until the coal-bright ember
Drifts up past brush and I
Return numb with knowing
Of yet more hours to come
Casting cedar, only to hear
Some other color calling
Distinct and distant – the
Luck and luxury of gold
Glaze flickering to flourish
In air before the rouge
Could be hastily fixed upon
The blue blush of sky.

Lady's Slipper

Tiny zeppelins tethered
To leafless stems;
Blousy bellows
Heralding summer;
Alternatively labeled
Moccasin Flower,
Whippoorwill Shoe,
Or Princess' Sandal;
Exquisitely frail,
A pink extravagance
Amid the dappled
Shade of birch, pine
Barren, or perhaps
The quilted thrum
Of brooks; enticing
Bees into voluptuous
Blossoms — pollen-
Poachers, they're denied
Reward since nectar's
A treasure taken
Or in short supply.
Yet there's a price
For terrestrial fragility:
Flamboyant bouffant,
Slow-growing lung,
Difficult to transplant
Or to coax towards
Something other than
A diminishing habitat.

Lupines

Colonies of color,
Clustered in full-
Knuckled thrust,
Blue dominant,
Dark as cobalt
Or a paler shade
Appearing bleached
By draught.
Hand-bell shakers,
Carbuncled thumbs,
Cylinders knotted
With flanged spires;
Fragrant vessels of
Silence bearing
Early summer light.
Deep-taprooted,
Eased from frost
And long oblivion,
They extend feathered
Fists, shaking an
Outwashed earth
From its cold sleep.

The Way of Willows

They seem at once ethereal
And earthbound; a vertical puddle
That is the misbegotten element
Of water and air or else ample
Adjectives amid the hefty nouns
Of oak and sheer verb of birch.
Within their haunt of pale-green
Mesh, no branch bends bare and
Even the young shoots lilt. Ever
Absorbing and emitting light,
They come to assume the shapes
Of those they shelter: falling now
Like sloths shuddering down
To water; flocks of finches –
Green-yellow-gold – in luminous
Clutter and holding hard to air;
Tangled merlettes flailing or
Castanets rustling in leaf-soft drizzle
Until wind lets up and each hush
Of branch falls to light like filament.

Crocuses

Small bundled bodies,
Parishes of purple dust,
Snow-crusted
And winter drowsy.

Their tiny husks
Of canary yellow
Or topaz likely fueled
Their brute petal thrust

Towards sun.
Their peacock displays
Eschew subtlety:
The dress is homespun

Lunging towards lush.
Even frost fails to deter
Their want of air.
Or their dreamward rush.

Dandelion

Lion's Tooth, sulfur-yellow tam of tuft
Holding horizontal like a small
Brocade set atop a hollow stem,
I watch your virus-quick transformation
From tasseled floret to ghost, a soft
Orb of seed, gossamer halo, tiny
Translucent moon of grandeur that
Is unmoored from a nest of coarse,
Serrated leaf and, breaking huddle,
Is taken up by wind bearing your
Ravenous progeny and their innate
Lust for land, setting forth as light
As breath to probe and place
Bearded bristles – treble hooks –
That bleed into taproots the size
Of small snakes, descending
Deeply down to a cooler earth,
Before fever spreads like a rash
Across the green flesh of grass.
Miracle weed, your blotched
And buttery folds, low and land-
Locked, still heal us with a verdant
Balm of latex and iodine.

Irises

Whispers have flowered forth
And fashioned you from wind;
The purpling of ocean froth
Lisps cursive and forms your skin.

Your jewel-bright embellishments
Rush to richness,
Tongues of dew-soft filament
Long and lovely and lush.

The refined majesty,
The whimsical swallowing
And effortless mastery
Of making light sing.

In bright and blousy fluency
Temperate air transforms to sea.

Wisteria

To our ineloquent eyes, they appeared as purple
Parachutes, tiny pouches buoyant from a wind
That eased into each cavity
With the grace of some divinity;

A profusion of petals that whirled
In savage sweetness, perpetually descending
In a thickly tangled canopy
Of feathered shadows and gnarled vines.

And, indeed, for a time,
Such luxury seemed never-ending,
For even after the last of honeysuckle –
Our abandoned sanctuary

Of perfumed abundance in decline –
We'd seek out these wisteria bowers bent
With tiny astonishments: a purpling
Of air fused in haphazard luxury.

There, for certain, no person could divine
Our hermitage, save the wind
And the disheveled light that filtered in
Before the fragrant darkening.

Honey Harvest

Rising late from ambered sleep
Drinking in the scent of honey-apple air,
Drowsy arms and hands would keep
The pleasured hum within my ear.

The stove heaves and crackles fire
The barn is bruised to burnished gold,
Woodsmoke and cider swiftly conspire
To make sweet musk of autumn cold.

In white lament, the netting foams
To tender awning about the eyes;
Now to bee box and bloom of combs
Where thudding tongues of haunted hives

Rise in a curled and luminous cloud
Scruffing at air with drizzled wing;
Their teeming groans speed to loud
And gloves give way to whistling sting.

Oily sheathings are born to light,
Perhaps the very fire that leaps
From star to star on moonless nights.
Root-cooled and autumn deep,

The faraway garden gasps for breath
Bunkered in blankets of plum and brown.
Unbidden here their tender death
And sacrament sucked from giving ground.

The barn bellows and calls us home;
Liquid vials loom and fill our eyes;
In pollen clouds of blurred moan,
The voice of light and fragrant skies.

IL MARE

Low Tide at Dawn

In pearl-blue rolling
The tongue of chimes
On sea-scented wind;

Pink blossoming
Of sky refines
The shore's tin

Glaze. Silt blending
With drowsy tides,
Beach is grafted

To linen. Back pedaling
Of waves to brine-
Blackened

Pools. Wide-winged
Egrets glide
To an abandoned

Sandspit; a feathering
Of cloud slides
Past; they're dawn-

Dappled
In sun, and help define
Where water ends
And land begins.

Summer Wind

His pallid face rises from a gritty
Pillow of salt and gravel;
Hard-drinking wind staggers
Towards a seething shore. Silk jacket
Torn, shirt tail swelling
With incoming tides, he sits
Shoeless, hair tasseled,
Glistening gold with sand,
Seeking equilibrium on land.

Head still heavy with dream
And lavish banquets of watery light,
The dulcet cadence of the Hesperides,
Pink-thinning suns and soft-mouthed seas,
Undulating swells of whitest
Gold coupling in drowsy delirium
With a gibbous moon delighting
In its own precious light, even
As darkness fills the vault of heaven.

Sun-struck, tossed up to savage
Shore, listless, he is pulled back to sleep.
Wind dozes, a force afflicted.
Rising, his broken body lifts,
Is taken back into the deep,
Wounded, sand-crusted,
Hearing the static-sharp shrieks
Of low-flying gulls, phantoms laughing
At his inevitable convulsion and collapse.

Chanson de la Nuit

Moon skims the horizon
Like a flat stone kissed
By water, only later rising
Dripping brightness,

A guilder that's been flipped
Upon its side, rolling
Westward, as if inhibited
From a more celestial calling.

Eventually gravity slips,
Night drifts down to dawn.
Within her gladdening grip,
Waves fall to fawning.

So, another day's begun;
We worship a second sun.

I Mean to Be a Watcher of Tides

I mean to be a watcher of tides,
Silver-blue waves buckling
And rolling like wide
Flatcars rumbling
Into a railyard. Tethered
Boats, sun-dappled, rock
Drowsily. Deep to ear,
The harbor's horn –
A bassoon's low moan –
Gives voice to air.
Gulls, wind-ushered, glide
By like a squadron
In fixed form, banking
Towards a weathered pier.

It is difficult to discern
If the waves are bearing
Or creating light. Layering
Of milky slosh churns
To froth; glistening
Particles of sand, dried
To silt by sun, burn
Molten gold resembling
Tiny coins. Channels
Run gray to amber
Until egrets return
In their gliding
Clouds of cream-
White flaring.

AFTER-WORDS

Kestrel

after Gerard Manley Hopkins

Heart near bursting, resplendent annunciation,
Blue-grey salutation and voluptous ravishing,
Wing-tips funneled, ineffable glistening
In vernal vestment, hope incarnate
Ushered from effulgent air, blowsy brown chestnut,
At Eastertide.

Vanquisher of despair, chalice of moon-gold crust
Glory-be aspergillum, sunlight's opulent dust
Glistening, carillon in dew-struck crepuscular
Archangel's ablution and healing breath.
Fatal flames forge a new, eternal covenant,
Tidings

Froth in wet enamel sheen. Up and up brightest
Wings burnished – cloud-crumpled flight,
Inimitable lapis, feather blush triumphant
Pyre rising with sudden, seraphic sword –
Oh, deliverer of salvation, falling upwards
Towards green skies.

Winter Passage

after Wallace Stevens

Perched upon the fence, thirteen crows
Like whole notes set out upon a staff,
On the corner post, a clef of snow

Hardened by ice. A branch of birch now
Rises and gothic wings extend as if
Preparing for song or flight, although

Wind proves a poor conductor, and so
The brute murder combusts and shifts
From nuanced phrasing into a show

Of ravaged fusion: sounds at once slow
And manic, rasps and chafes.
Notes arch and pour with abandon. Now

Song and silence somehow coalesce –
What approaches ear recedes also.

Sonnet

after William Shakespeare (Sonnet LXXIII)

The season of hope and harvest past,
All the world now appears winter white
With a cold, uneasy silence cast
And a nearer darkness. All light's
Fractured but for that knotted stand
Of river birch glazed with ice: wind-
Battered branches, like empty hands,
Haphazardly sway while lower boughs bend
With an enameled clutch of lemon yellow
Leaves. So, love, would I extend to you,
Even as all things diminish and time slows,
Such an offering: a second-self renewed
And the near-certain promise that brings
Forgiveness and the hope of life everlasting.

Nature's First Gold

after Robert Frost

Nature's first gold is green;
Yellow wanes between.
And so we mark the passing
Of what will be and what has been.

Life burns brightest near its end,
Arcs to zenith, and then
Will wither until its very last
Light's expended.

Enlighten Our Darkness, Lady

(Illumina tenebras nostras domina)

after John Donne

Then, as the moon holds steadfast
And keeps an eternal eye,
Even when, in darker phases cast,
Or when the soft paling of the sky

Lightens our darkness, love,
It still, in cold elliptic, holds
As the seas will justly prove,
Rising or falling with their moods.

A thing eclipsing, angels see
That absence brings comfort
In the grace of your gravity:
Though it serves to distort

My sphere, a distended circle's just,
For in you, I forsake my wanderlust.

Autumn

after John Keats

I

This haunted season settles
And dissolves into mists;
Frosted leaves, too, ripen and fall;
Bloom-hung, red and yellow chrysalis.
Lisp of bees and swallows call —
Tawny blurs of bliss —
Gathering just before the lull
That falls between dusk and emptiness.

II

The fragrance of the harvest
Lingers sweetly still;
Across Autumn's lap the scythe rests,
Hem furling. An ancient granary is filled
With bushels brightly blessed:
Hazel nuts, fruits and wine, deeply chilled,
Cups brimming with purpled drowsiness
That pours to tongue like feathered light.

III

Sun-dappled spring is now a season past
And winter's burden further on abides;
Daylight draws down and casts

A temperate and softening light
Redolent with hay and fresh-mown grass;
At pasture's edge, a fertile garden bright
With the cloudy rush of sage and aster –
The timbre of twilight.

IV

Memory too stirs and wakens momentarily;
Haunted by the honey'd warmth of the sun,
She turns with such seduction steadily
Towards softer, dying days begun
In rich indolence that empty and fill
Each moment with luster and a clear under-
Standing of what has been freely
Lost and what more is forthcoming.

ABOUT THE AUTHOR

A life-long resident of Connecticut, John Muro is a graduate of Trinity College in Hartford. He has also attained advanced degrees from Wesleyan University and the University of Connecticut. He has been an advocate for environmental stewardship and conservation throughout his career, and he has held several volunteer and executive positions in those fields. He has had a life-long passion for literature and the arts, and considers himself particularly fortunate to have worked at The Wadsworth Atheneum, the Bushnell Memorial and the Hartford Stage Company (all in Hartford) while a student. John has been recognized for his volunteer activities by the State of Connecticut, and he has also been recognized by the U.S. Small Business Administration and the U.S. Chamber of Commerce for his efforts in support of small businesses. John was a resident of Bolton, CT, until he recently relocated to Guilford on the Connecticut shoreline with his wife, Debra Ann. They have four children. This is his first volume of published poems.

This book is set in Garamond Premier Pro, which had its genesis in 1988 when type-designer Robert Slimbach visited the Plantin-Moretus Museum in Antwerp, Belgium, to study its collection of Claude Garamond's metal punches and typefaces. During the mid-fifteen hundreds, Garamond—a Parisian punch-cutter—produced a refined array of book types that combined an unprecedented degree of balance and elegance, for centuries standing as the pinnacle of beauty and practicality in type-founding. Slimbach has created an entirely new interpretation based on Garamond's designs and on compatible italics cut by Robert Granjon, Garamond's contemporary.

For more concerning the work of John Muro, visit
www.antrimhousebooks.com/authors.html
This book is available at all bookstores
including Amazon.